AF765608

MARIO JORDAN

The Power Of The Mind

Co-Creating Your Reality

MARIO JORDAN

Copyright © 2025 by Mario Jordan

All rights reserved. No part of this publication may be reproduced, stored or transmitted in any form or by any means, electronic, mechanical, photocopying, recording, scanning, or otherwise without written permission from the publisher. It is illegal to copy this book, post it to a website, or distribute it by any other means without permission.

Mario Jordan asserts the moral right to be identified as the author of this work.

First edition

This book was professionally typeset on Reedsy.
Find out more at reedsy.com

This book is dedicated to every seeker who ever felt there must be more to life, to every dreamer who dared to imagine a better reality, and to every warrior who continues to show up and do the work of transformation. May you remember your true power and create a life that takes your breath away.

The Mind, your mind, is so powerful ✨ you can literally shift dimensions and realities.... the power lies within you

— Mario Jordan

Contents

Foreword

The Awakening

There is a secret sleeping in plain sight, hidden in the most obvious place imaginable, within your own mind. For centuries, mystics have whispered about it, philosophers have pondered it, and now, quantum physicists are proving it: your reality is not fixed. It is malleable. You are not merely a passenger on the journey of your life; you are its chief architect.

This book is the key to unlocking that secret. It is a declaration that the power you have been seeking externally has been within you all along, waiting to be recognized and harnessed. We are living in a time of great awakening, where the lines between science and spirituality are blurring, revealing a profound truth: we are co-creators, in constant dialogue with the universe.

What you hold in your hands is more than a book; it is a guide to the most sophisticated technology you will ever own: the human mind. It is a practical manual for taking back control of your inner world so that your outer world can transform in response. The journey we are about to embark on will take us deep into the landscapes of consciousness, from the logical mind to the vast, powerful subconscious, all the way to the infinite field of intelligence that connects us all.

The era of feeling like a victim of circumstance is over. The era of conscious creation begins now. Take a deep breath, turn the page, and let the awakening commence.

Preface

This book was born from a place of deep frustration and an even deeper knowing.

For years, I felt like I was living a life designed by someone else. I was following the script: go to school, get a good job, be practical, yet I felt a constant, nagging sense that there was more. I watched as some people seemed to effortlessly create the lives of their dreams, while others, including myself at times, seemed to work tirelessly only to remain stuck in the same cycles of lack, frustration, and unfulfilled potential.

I began to ask a simple, powerful question: Why?

This question launched me on a decades-long quest. I devoured everything I could find: from ancient spiritual texts to cutting-edge neuroscience, from the esoteric teachings of mystics to the practical frameworks of modern psychologists. I became a bio-hacker of my own consciousness, testing every principle, technique, and theory on the one and only subject I had full access to: myself.

What I discovered was not a secret hidden in a remote ashram or a complex formula accessible only to geniuses. I found a universal operating system, a set of fundamental laws that govern how we shape our reality. I learned that the difference between those who manifest their dreams and those who don't isn't luck, privilege, or destiny. It is understanding. It is the understanding of how to harness the triune power of the mind and align it with the creative intelligence of the universe.

This book is the distillation of everything I learned. It is the guide I wish I had when I started. It is a practical, no-nonsense manual that bridges the gap between the mystical and the scientific, between wishful thinking and demonstrated results.

You are not broken. You do not need fixing. You only need to remember who you are and learn to use the incredible power that has been within you all along. Approach this book with an open mind and a willing heart. Do the exercises. Apply the principles. Your life is about to change.

Acknowledgments

A book may have a single name on the cover, but it is always the product of a chorus of support, wisdom, and love.

First, I must acknowledge the countless sages, scientists, and teachers upon whose shoulders I stand. The work of pioneers like Dr. Joe Dispenza, Dr. Bruce Lipton, Carl Jung, and many others provided the foundational stones upon which this book is built. My deepest gratitude for your courage to explore the frontiers of human potential.

To my clients and students, who have been my greatest teachers. Your courage to confront your own shadows, your willingness to do the work, and your incredible transformations have been the living proof of these principles. Thank you for trusting me to guide you and for teaching me more than you can ever know.

To my unwavering agent and insightful editor, who saw the potential in this manuscript and tirelessly helped me sculpt it into its best form. Your belief in this message kept me going when doubt crept in.

To my cherished friends and family, who endured my distracted presence during the long months of writing and rewriting. Thank you for the cups of tea left quietly on my desk, for the words of encouragement, and for forgiving my occasional absence. Your love is the bedrock of my life.

Prologue

The Last Day of Your Old Life

Imagine for a moment that tonight, as you sleep, a silent switch is flipped. The person you are today: with all their doubts, their limitations, their repeating problems, will gently dissolve. Tomorrow, you will wake up as the most powerful version of yourself.

How would that feel?

What if you knew, with unshakable certainty, that you could achieve any goal you set? What if your mind was a focused laser of creativity, your body a vessel of vibrant health, and your life a canvas for joy and abundance? What if every relationship was a source of nourishment and every challenge a stepping stone to greater strength?

This is not a fantasy. This is your birthright.

The fact that you can even conceive of this possibility is proof that it exists within you. That version of you is not a future self you need to build from scratch. It is your essential self, waiting to be uncovered.

The pages that follow are the map to that uncovering. They contain the instructions for operating the most sophisticated technology in the known universe: your own consciousness. This knowledge will demand something of you. It will demand that you take full responsibility for your reality. It will require you to look, with unflinching honesty, at the programs you've been running and find the courage to rewrite them.

But the reward is everything. It is your freedom. It is your power. It is your life, lived on your terms.

Consider this your final moment as the old you. Take a deep breath. Turn the page. Let’s begin.

Introduction

The Remembering

I want you to think back to a time in your childhood when your imagination was vivid and real. A time when you could become a pirate sailing treacherous seas, an astronaut exploring distant galaxies, or a princess ruling a magical kingdom. In those moments, your imagined reality felt tangible. There was no doubt, no skepticism, only pure, creative belief.

Somewhere along the way, most of us lost that. We were taught to "be realistic," to "grow up," and to accept the "real world." We traded our innate creative power for societal approval and security. But that power never left you. It merely went dormant, waiting for you to remember it.

This book is about that remembering.

It is about recalling that you are, and always have been, a powerful creator. Every single thing in our man-made world: the device you're reading this on, the chair you're sitting in, the building around you, began as a thought in someone's consciousness. That thought was nurtured, believed in, and acted upon until it solidified into physical form. This process is not magic; it is the fundamental mechanism of creation, and it is available to you right now.

We will explore the science and the soul of this process. We will demystify the laws that govern reality and provide you with a practical, step-by-step framework for applying them. This is not about positive thinking alone; it is about positive being. It is about aligning every level of your consciousness:

your thoughts, your beliefs, your emotions, and your actions, with the reality you wish to experience.

The path of a co-creator is one of profound personal responsibility and even more profound personal power. It requires courage to examine your deepest programming and the discipline to rewrite it. But the reward is a life of purpose, joy, and freedom: a life that is truly your own.

You are about to remember who you are and what you are capable of. Let's begin.

I

THE TRIUNE MIND – UNDERSTANDING YOUR INNER UNIVERSE 🌀

Before you can command the ship, you must know your crew. This section unveils the three layers of your consciousness: the Conscious Mind, the Captain who sets the intention; the Subconscious Mind, the powerful Autopilot running your habits and beliefs; and the Super-conscious Mind, the infinite Ocean of universal intelligence you sail upon. Understanding their dynamic is the first step to mastering your reality.

1

The Conscious Mind: The Captain 🧠

Meet the Captain of your ship. This is the part of you that is aware of reading these words. Your conscious mind is your identity: the thinker, the analyzer, the decision-maker. It is the voice in your head that narrates your experience, weighs options, and exercises willpower.

The Captain's primary functions are crucial for navigation:

Logic and Analysis: It processes information linearly, solving problems and making logical decisions. "If I save this amount each month, I can afford that vacation."

Short-Term Memory: It holds temporary information, like a grocery list or a phone number, before either discarding it or transferring it to long-term storage.

Willpower and Volition: It initiates action based on conscious choice. "I will start meditating today." "I will not check my phone during dinner."

The Captain's greatest power is its ability to set intention. This is the first and most critical step in creation. By declaring, "I am moving toward a life of vibrant health," or "I am creating a successful and purposeful business," the

Captain points the ship in a specific direction. Without a conscious destination, the ship drifts aimlessly, subject to every current and wind.

However, the Captain has significant limitations. It is easily overwhelmed. Think of it as having a very small desk that can only hold a few pieces of paper at a time. When too much information piles up: stress from work, relationship worries, financial pressures etc, the Captain becomes fatigued, distracted, and prone to making poor decisions. Its willpower is a finite resource that depletes throughout the day, which is why you might resist a donut in the morning but succumb to ice cream at night.

Most importantly, the Captain is not in charge of the ship's engines or its deep-seated navigation charts. It can give the order "Full speed ahead to Abundance!" but if the crew in the engine room: your subconscious mind, has a different map, the order will be ignored, or the ship will mysteriously develop "engine trouble." The Captain is essential for setting the course, but it cannot steer the ship alone.

Practical Exercise: The Intention Setter

For the next seven days, before you get out of bed, set a clear and positive intention for your day. Don't just think it; speak it aloud.

"Today, my intention is to move through my day with peace and purpose."
"Today, my intention is to see the best in everyone I meet."
"Today, my intention is to take one concrete step toward my goal."

This simple practice strengthens the Captain's authority, training it to choose your direction consciously, rather than simply reacting to the day's events.

2

The Subconscious Mind: The Autopilot✈

Beneath the deck, in the deep holds of your ship, works the most powerful crew member: your subconscious mind. This is the Autopilot, the Chief Engineer, and the Head Librarian all in one. It is millions of times more powerful than the conscious mind in processing capacity, and it never, ever sleeps.

The subconscious is responsible for:

Running Your Body: It controls your heartbeat, digestion, breathing, and every other autonomic function without your conscious effort.

Long-Term Memory Storage: It is the vast library of your entire life experience, storing every sight, sound, feeling, and smell.

The Habit Center: It operates on programmed routines. Brushing your teeth, driving a car, your knee-jerk emotional reactions, these are all subconscious programs running automatically for efficiency.

The Seat of Emotion: Emotions are the native language of the subconscious.

The most critical thing to understand about the subconscious is that it is not logical; it is impressionable. It accepts whatever the conscious mind repeatedly thinks and feels as absolute truth. It is a faithful servant that follows orders without judgment.

How the Programming Happens:

The primary programming occurs between birth and approximately age seven. During this time, a child's brain operates predominantly in theta waves, a hypnotic, highly suggestible state. This is a biological design for rapid learning, but it means the child absorbs everything: beliefs, behaviors, traumas, and words without a filter.

If you heard, "Money doesn't grow on trees," your subconscious may have recorded it as "Money is scarce."

If a parent was frequently critical, you may have internalized "I'm not good enough."

If you witnessed conflict in relationships, you may have stored "Love is painful."

These impressions become the "maps" your subconscious uses to navigate the world. The Captain can shout a new destination, but the Autopilot will always, always follow its pre-installed map. This is the root of self-sabotage. You consciously want success, but your subconscious map of unworthiness creates "engine trouble": procrastination, imposter syndrome, and missed opportunities.

The good news is profound: the maps can be redrawn. The programs can be rewritten. The first step is to bring them into the light.

Practical Exercise: The Belief Detective

Take a notebook and for one week, become a detective of your own thoughts. Pay attention to your automatic responses, especially when you feel a strong negative emotion.

When you make a mistake, what do you immediately think? ("I'm so stupid.")

When you see someone very successful, what's your internal reaction? ("They're so lucky; that could never be me.")

When you think about your dreams, what fears arise? ("Who am I to think I could do that?")

Write these thoughts down without judgment. You are not your thoughts; you are the observer of your thoughts. This list is your first glimpse at the old maps your Autopilot has been using.

3

The Super-Conscious Mind: The Infinite Ocean 🌊

Now, let's step back from the ship itself and look at where it is sailing. Your ship does not travel through an empty void. It sails upon a vast, intelligent, and infinitely creative Ocean. This is your super-conscious mind: also known as Universal Intelligence, Source, God, or the Quantum Field.

The Super-conscious is not a personal mind like the conscious and subconscious; it is the universal mind that connects all things. It is the source of all inspiration, true genius, synchronicity, and what we might call "miracles."

Its characteristics are:

Infinite Intelligence and Knowing: It is the source of "downloads" and "aha!" moments. The solution to a problem that suddenly pops into your head, the song that a composer "hears" fully formed, this is the Super-conscious communicating.

Interconnectedness: It orchestrates life's "coincidences." You think of an old friend, and they call minutes later. You need a specific resource, and you "randomly" meet the perfect person. This is the Ocean's intelligent organization at work.

Pure Potentiality: Within the Super-conscious Ocean, every possible reality exists as a potential waveform. Your desire for a loving partner, a healing body, or a purposeful career already exists there as a seed of potential.

The "Co" in Co-Creation:

True creation is not a solo act of willpower. It is a divine partnership. Here is how the trinity works together:

1. The Captain (Conscious Mind) sets the intention: "I am sailing toward the Island of Vibrant Health."

2. The Autopilot (Subconscious Mind) must be reprogrammed with a new map that believes this is possible and feels the feelings of already being healthy. This creates internal alignment.

3. When the Captain and Autopilot are in harmony: when your conscious desires and subconscious beliefs are a match, you drop your anchor into the Super-conscious Ocean.

This alignment opens a clear channel. The power and intelligence of the Universe can now flow through you effortlessly. It provides the perfect winds (synchronicity), guides you to safe harbors (opportunities), and makes the journey not a struggle, but a joyful, flowing adventure. You are no longer rowing; you are sailing.

Your primary work as a co-creator is to achieve and maintain this internal alignment. The Universe handles the rest.

Practical Exercise: Tuning In

Once a day, find a quiet moment. Close your eyes and take three deep breaths.

Ask a simple, open-ended question into the silence, such as:

"What do I need to know today for my highest good?"

"Show me the next step toward my goal."

Don't force an answer. Just listen. You might receive a word, an image, a memory, or a feeling of peace. This is the beginning of your conscious communication with the Ocean. Trust what you receive.

II

THE REPROGRAMMING – TAKING BACK CONTROL 🩹

Your current reality is a printout of your past programming. To change the output, you must change the software. This part is your practical guide to rewiring your brain and reprogramming your subconscious. Through proven techniques like bio-hacking, visualization, and shadow work, you will learn to overwrite limiting beliefs and install new, empowering programs of success and abundance.

4

The Art of Bio-Hacking Your Brain 🧠

Your brain is not a static organ; it is malleable and adaptable, a quality known as neuroplasticity. Every thought you think carves a neural pathway. The more you think that thought, the deeper and more automatic the pathway becomes. "Bio-hacking" is the conscious and deliberate practice of rewiring these pathways to optimize your mind's performance. You are quite literally upgrading your internal hardware to run your new software.

Hack #1: Meditation – The System Update

Meditation is the single most powerful tool for quieting the busy Captain and accessing the programmable state of the Autopilot. It shifts your brainwaves from high-frequency beta (active thinking) to calmer alpha (relaxed focus) and theta (deep meditation, hypnosis). In the theta state, you can communicate directly with your subconscious and install new programs.

The Practice: Start with just 10 minutes. Sit comfortably, close your eyes, and focus on your breath. When your mind wanders (and it will), gently guide it back to the breath. That act of noticing and returning is the practice: it strengthens your conscious mind's ability to focus and choose its thoughts. For a more targeted approach, try guided meditations designed for manifestation or subconscious reprogramming.

Hack #2: Breathwork – The Remote Control

Your breath is a direct line to your autonomic nervous system. You can use it to switch from a state of stress (sympathetic, fight-or-flight) to a state of calm (parasympathetic, rest-and-digest) in minutes. A stressed brain is a closed brain, incapable of learning or creating new pathways.

The 4-7-8 Technique: Inhale through your nose for a count of 4. Hold your breath for a count of 7. Exhale slowly through your mouth for a count of 8. Repeat this cycle 4-6 times. This technique is a powerful anxiolytic, instantly signaling safety to your subconscious.

Hack #3: Nutrition & Sleep – The High-Octane Fuel

You cannot run high-vibrational software on low-quality fuel. A brain inflamed by sugar and processed foods and deprived of sleep is a foggy, reactive brain stuck in survival mode.

Nutrition: Focus on whole foods, plenty of healthy fats (your brain is 60% fat!), and hydration. Omega-3s, found in fish and flax seeds, are particularly crucial for brain cell health.

Sleep: During deep sleep, your brain cleanses itself of metabolic toxins and consolidates learning into long-term memory. Prioritize 7-9 hours of quality sleep. It is non-negotiable for mental and physical regeneration.

5

Rewiring the Subconscious 💭

Now we get to the core of the work: overwriting the old, limiting software in your Autopilot. This requires consistency, emotion, and repetition.

Technique #1: Affirmations with Emotional Fuel

Affirmations are new, positive, present-tense statements that you consciously choose to replace the old ones. The key is not just the words, but the feeling behind them.

Craft Them Correctly: They must be:

Present Tense: "I am confident and capable," not "I will be confident."

Positive: "I am healthy and vibrant," not "I am not sick."

Believable: If "I am a millionaire" feels like a lie, start with "I am opening myself to abundant streams of income."

Prime Time: The best times to program your subconscious are right before you fall asleep and right after you wake up, when you are in a theta-dominant state. Repeat your affirmations with strong feeling for 5 minutes at these times. Feel the joy, the gratitude, the confidence as if it's already true.

Technique #2: Visualization – Neurological Rehearsal

Your subconscious thinks in pictures and sensations. Vivid visualization is not daydreaming; it is neurological rehearsal that primes your brain to recognize and create opportunities in the physical world.

Your Daily Mental Movie: Close your eyes and spend 10-15 minutes vividly imagining your desired reality. If it's your dream home, don't just see it: walk through the front door. Feel the texture of the counter-top. Smell the coffee brewing. Hear the laughter of your family. See yourself living there, feeling happy, secure, and grateful.

Embody the Emotion: This is the command that tells your subconscious and the Universe, "This is my reality." The feeling of accomplishment is more important than the visual details.

Technique #3: Subliminal Programming

This involves bypassing the conscious critic entirely. You can listen to audio tracks where positive affirmations are masked by music or nature sounds, or you can record your own affirmations and play them at a low volume while you sleep. Your conscious ear won't hear them, but your subconscious will absorb them directly.

6

Shadow Work: Integrating Your Hidden Self

Your "shadow" is a concept popularized by Carl Jung, representing the parts of yourself you have repressed, denied, or hidden away, often because you learned they were "bad," "unacceptable," or "shameful." This can include anger, jealousy, fear, greed, or past traumas.

These disowned parts don't disappear; they are stored in the subconscious and run your life from the shadows. They manifest as projections (seeing traits you dislike in others), triggers (over-the-top emotional reactions), and self-sabotaging patterns.

Shadow work is the courageous process of bringing these hidden parts into the light of your conscious awareness, not to eliminate them, but to understand and integrate them. This reclaims immense power that was being used to keep them hidden.

The Shadow Work Process:

1. Identify a Trigger: When you have a strong negative reaction to someone or something, pause. Ask yourself: "What is it about this that bothers me so much?"

2. Own the Projection: Recognize that the intense charge means you are likely seeing a disowned part of yourself. If you are furious at someone for being "irresponsible," you may be repressing your own desire to be more carefree.

3. Dialogue with Compassion: In your journal, have a conversation with this shadow part. "Anger, why are you here? What are you trying to protect me from?" Listen without judgment. You may find that your repressed anger is trying to protect you from being taken advantage of.

4. Integrate and Thank: Acknowledge that this part of you has served a purpose. Thank it for its protection, and then consciously choose a new, more empowered way to meet that need. "Thank you, Anger, for protecting my boundaries. I now choose to set clear and loving boundaries instead."

Integrating your shadow is perhaps the most profound work you can do. It ends internal civil war and makes you whole, allowing all of your energy to be directed toward conscious creation.

III

THE SCIENCE & ART OF MANIFESTATION 🎨

🖌

Creation is not magic; it is a precise formula. Here, we move from theory to practice, detailing the step-by-step process of turning thought into tangible reality. You will master the shift from the vibration of "wanting" to the powerful "knowing," learn to take inspired action, and embrace the art of surrender to partner with the universe in bringing your desires to life.

7

The Manifestation Formula

Manifestation is the natural result of a mind that is fully aligned. It is the process of bringing the invisible into the visible. The formula is sequential and governed by immutable laws.

Step 1: Thought (The Seed)

Every creation begins with a conscious idea. "I want a loving relationship." "I am building a successful business." This is the Captain setting the destination.

Step 2: Emotion (The Fuel)

You must attach a feeling to the thought. Excitement, passion, joy, gratitude. This emotional charge is what gives the thought its creative power. It sends a powerful command to your subconscious and a clear signal to the Quantum Field. A thought without emotion is like a seed without water; it will not grow.

Step 3: Vibration (The Broadcast)

Your emotional state emits a specific frequency, like a radio tower. The Law of Attraction is simply the law of resonance: you attract what you are in vibrational harmony with. If you feel poor and desperate, you vibrate at the frequency of lack, attracting more lack. If you feel grateful and abundant, you vibrate at the frequency of abundance, attracting more abundance. Your dominant vibration is your request to the universe.

Step 4: Manifestation (The Harvest)

Your sustained vibration pulls corresponding people, opportunities, and resources into your physical reality. The perfect client calls, you find the ideal apartment, you meet a kindred spirit. This is not magic; it is the universe efficiently organizing itself around your energetic signature.

The entire process depends on the alignment between your conscious thought (Step 1) and your subconscious feeling (Step 2). If they conflict, your vibration will be mixed, and your results will be inconsistent.

8

The State of Knowing vs. Wanting 🧘‍♀️

This is the quantum leap in manifestation. You must shift from the hope of the future to the faith of the present.

The State of Wanting (Vibration of Lack):

"I hope I get that promotion."
"I wish I could find my soulmate."
"I need to get out of debt."

This language comes from a place of not having. It screams "I DON'T HAVE THIS!" to the universe, which obediently continues to reflect that lack back to you. Wanting reaffirms the absence of your desire.

The State of Knowing (Vibration of Having):

"I am so grateful for my new role and its increased abundance."
"I am open and ready to welcome my soulmate."
"Money flows to me easily and frequently."

This comes from a place of already being it. It feels like a fact. You live, act, and feel as if your desire is already fulfilled. You don't hope for it; you know it is done. This is the state that commands the universe to deliver.

How to Cultivate the State of Knowing:

Act As If: Dress, speak, and organize your life as if you are already the person who has your desire.

Practice Gratitude: Feel genuine gratitude for your desire as if it has already been granted. This is the most powerful vibration you can emit.

Release the "How": Trust that the universe has a thousand ways to bring you your desire that your conscious mind cannot conceive of. Your job is to hold the vibration; the universe's job is to handle the delivery.

9

Inspired Action & Divine Surrender ◉

Co-creation is a dance between your effort and the universe's flow. You must take action, but the quality of that action is everything.

Inspired Action vs. Forced Action:

Forced Action is born of anxiety and lack. It's pushing, striving, and trying to make it happen from your limited conscious mind alone. It feels heavy, exhausting, and comes from the belief "It's all up to me."

Inspired Action is light, joyful, and intuitive. It's the nudge to call an old friend, to sign up for a class, to write an email. This is the Super-conscious Ocean guiding you. It feels like flow, synchronicity, and right timing. It emerges naturally from the State of Knowing.

The Art of Divine Surrender:

After you have set your intention, programmed your subconscious, and taken your inspired actions, you must let go. Surrender your attachment to the how and the when.

This is not passive resignation; it is active trust. It is saying, "I have done my part, and I now trust the intelligence of the universe to do its part in the perfect way and timing."

Surrender is the ultimate act of faith. It releases the tension of control and allows the magic of the universe to work through you. Watch for the synchronicities, the open doors, and the "lucky breaks" that appear when you release your grip.

IV

LIVING AS A CONSCIOUS CO-CREATOR ✧?

Mastery is not a one-time event, but a daily practice. This final section integrates all you have learned into a sustainable lifestyle. Discover the daily rituals of a co-creator, learn to navigate challenges with grace, and understand your ripple effect on the world. This is your guide to living permanently aligned with your power, transforming your life into an ongoing masterpiece of conscious creation.

10

The Daily Practice of a Co-Creator 🧘‍♂️ 🌀

Living as a co-creator is a lifestyle, maintained through consistent daily rituals. These practices keep your vibration high and your channel clear.

The Morning Ritual (Setting Your Vibration):

The first hour of your day is sacred. Do not let the outside world dictate your state. A sample ritual:

1. **Silence & Meditation (10-20 min):** Connect with your inner world before engaging with the outer world.

2. **Intentions & Affirmations (5 min):** Set your conscious direction for the day.

3. **Visualization (5-10 min):** Rehearse your desired reality.

4. **Gratitude Journaling (3 min):** Write down 3 things you're grateful for. This sets a frequency of abundance.

Throughout the Day (Mindful Maintenance):

Catch and Reframe: When a negative thought arises, catch it and reframe it. "This is challenging" becomes "This is an opportunity to grow."

Choose Your Emotion: You are the only one who can choose how you feel. When you feel yourself slipping into frustration or anxiety, pause, breathe, and consciously choose a better-feeling thought.

Follow the Nudge: When you get an inspired idea, act on it, no matter how small.

The Evening Review (Integration):

Reflect on your day without judgment. What went well? Where did you get off track? Acknowledge your progress and forgive your stumbles.

Before sleep, revisit your affirmations to program your subconscious overnight.

11

Navigating Challenges & Maintaining Alignment 🧘‍♂️

You will face challenges. The old patterns will try to reassert themselves. This is not a sign that you're failing; it's feedback that you're growing.

When You Feel Stuck or Out of Alignment:

1. **Return to the Breath:** Use breath-work to calm your nervous system immediately.

2. **Get into Vortex:** Do something that brings you pure joy: listen to music, dance, walk in nature, play with a pet. This raises your vibration instantly.

3. **Focus on What's Working:** Shift your attention from the problem to any small thing that is going right. This changes your point of attraction.

4. **Revisit Your "Why":** Connect back to the deep, emotional reason behind your desire. This re-ignites your fuel.

Dealing with Setbacks:

See setbacks as course corrections, not failures. They are often the universe redirecting you to something better. Ask, "What is this trying to teach me? How can I grow from this?" This alchemizes pain into power.

12

The Ripple Effect: Your Impact on the Collective 🌎

Your personal transformation is the most significant contribution you can make to the world. As you raise your vibration, you lift everyone around you.

Your peace becomes a sanctuary for others.

Your joy becomes contagious.

Your demonstrated ability to create your reality gives others permission to do the same.

You become a living example of what is possible. Without preaching, you inspire your family, your friends, and your community. This creates a ripple effect that elevates the collective consciousness. Healing yourself is the first step toward healing the world. Your journey to self-mastery is an act of profound service.

Conclusion: You Are the Universe Experiencing Itself

The journey we have taken is a homecoming. You are not a lonely, separate self trying to wrestle a better life from a resistant universe. You are an individualized expression of the universe itself, here to experience and create.

The power you sought was never outside of you. The Captain, the Autopilot, and the Ocean were always one: different aspects of the magnificent, creative consciousness that you are. The separation was the great illusion.

You now have the map and the tools. You understand the trinity of your mind and how to bring it into alignment. You know the formula for manifestation and the art of surrender. The rest is practice. It is showing up every day, choosing your thoughts, feeling your feelings, and taking inspired steps.

There will be days you feel perfectly aligned and days you feel lost. On both kinds of days, remember the truth: you are a co-creator. You are in a constant, dynamic dance with the intelligent universe. It is waiting for your command, ready to support you, guide you, and conspire in your favor.

The world is not as it is; it is as you are. As you continue to change your inner world, your outer world will transform in ways more beautiful and miraculous than you can currently imagine.

Go forth, and create a masterpiece.

13

Conclusion

The Architect of Your Dawn

We have journeyed far together, from the familiar shores of your conscious mind, through the deep and powerful waters of the subconscious, and out into the infinite expanse of the super-conscious ocean. You now hold the map. You understand the roles of the Captain, the Chief Engineer, and the vast Ocean itself. You are equipped with the tools to reprogram, rewire, and bio-hack your way into a new existence.

The theories, the formulas, the exercises, they are all now part of your toolkit. But remember this above all: Co-creation is a state of being, not a collection of techniques.

It is the daily practice of choosing your thoughts with intention, of feeling your feelings with purpose, and of acting from a place of inspired alignment. It is the profound shift from hoping something will happen to knowing it is already done, and then allowing the universe to orchestrate the details.

The life of your dreams is not a distant destination to be reached after years of struggle. It is a frequency to be tuned into, right here, right now. Every time you choose gratitude over complaint, faith over fear, or love over judgment, you are tuning that dial. Every time you pause to reset your vibration, you are stepping back into your power as the co-creator of your experience.

You are no longer a student of this work; you are a practitioner. You are no longer a dreamer; you are an architect. The blueprints are in your hands. The building materials are your thoughts, your beliefs, and your actions. The construction site is your present moment.

Go forth and build something magnificent.

Epilogue

A Letter from Your Future Self

Hi, self,

If you are reading this, it means you have absorbed the knowledge in this book. You have done the work. You have felt the shifts. Perhaps things have already begun to change in beautiful and unexpected ways. Or perhaps you are in a moment of pause, wondering if you can truly sustain this new way of being.

I am writing to you from a place you can now only imagine, but will soon know as home. I am your future self, living in the reality you are currently in the process of creating.

I want you to know that every single step you took was worth it. Every meditation, every affirmed statement, every moment you chose faith over fear: it all mattered. It all added up. The person you are becoming would astound the person who first picked up this book.

The challenges you faced did not break you; they forged you. The old patterns that tried to reassert themselves are now nothing but ghostly echoes, powerless memories of a life you no longer live. The joy, the peace, the abundance you cultivated internally have now blossomed into your external world in ways more perfect and creative than your past self could have ever planned.

I live in the house you visualized. I enjoy the fulfilling work you declared was yours. I share my life with the loving relationships you knew you deserved. But more than any external thing, I live with a feeling of unshakable peace and connectedness. I know, with every fiber of my being, that I am the source of my reality, in perfect partnership with a benevolent universe.

Keep going. Trust the process, especially when you cannot see the entire path. The universe is conspiring in your favor. I am the living proof.

With all my love,
The You That Was Always Meant to Be

Afterword

The Invitation

The final word of this book is not a period, but an invitation.

The knowledge you now possess is not meant to be shelved and admired. It is a living, breathing technology that demands application. It thrives on use and atrophies with neglect.

Your mission, should you choose to accept it, is to become a living testament to these principles. Let your life become the experiment. Let your transformation become the data. Let your joy become the conclusion.

This work does not end when you close this book; it begins. The true reading happens in the moments of your daily life: when you respond to a trigger with grace, when you spot an opportunity where others see obstacle, when you feel a deep sense of gratitude for no reason at all.

Share this knowledge, not necessarily by preaching, but by embodying it. As you change your world, you give everyone around you permission to change theirs. You become a beacon, a quiet revolution of one that has the power to uplift the collective.

The world needs your light, your unique creative expression, your healed and whole self. It is time to stop seeking permission and start living your truth.

The invitation is to create. The page is blank. The tools are in your hands.

What will you create first?

About the Author

Mario Jordan is a passionate voice in contemporary literature and advocacy, hailing from the beautiful island of Barbados. Drawing inspiration from his Caribbean roots and a deep concern for the human experience, his writing spans the vibrant realms of fantasy and the critical landscape of mental wellness.

He is the creative force behind the compelling fantasy novel "Dragon Heart", a tale that weaves together adventure, identity, and the enduring power of courage. Alongside his work in fiction, Mario is a dedicated advocate for mental health, channeling his insights into powerful, awareness-raising content that aims to de-stigmatize mental health challenges and foster a more compassionate and understanding world.

Mario believes in the power of stories, whether set in fantastical kingdoms or grounded in real-life struggles: to inspire, heal, and transform. His work, both in fiction and non-fiction, reflects his core belief in resilience, hope, and the strength of the human spirit.

When he isn't writing, Mario is a dedicated mentor in his community, using his platform to empower others and champion the importance of mental and emotional well-being.

www.ingramcontent.com/pod-product-compliance
Ingram Content Group UK Ltd.
Pitfield, Milton Keynes, MK11 3LW, UK
UKHW020124290926
15471UKWH00003B/259

9 798232 053284